We Meet At Moonlight

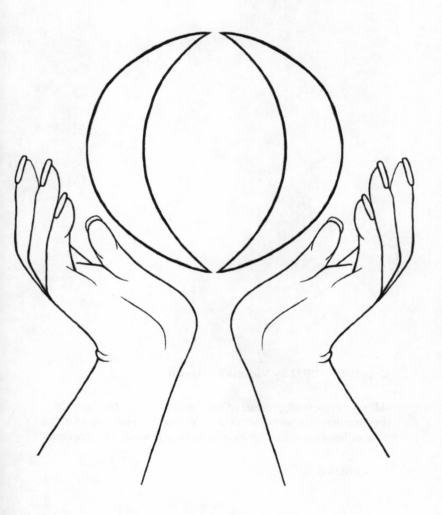

We Meet At Moonlight

Revised And Extended Edition

Victoria Pizzirusso

to those who have ripped out a heart
and left it for dead
i hope you find this.
i hope you find this and feel guilty.
i hope you find this and feel exposed.
i hope you find this and feel remorse.
i hope you find this and seek forgiveness.

to those who have been left
to bleed out of the hole in their chest
i hope you find this.
i hope you find this and feel seen.
i hope you find this and feel comfort.
i hope you find this and feel power.
i hope you find this and realize
you are all you will ever need.

*-please read this **out loud** and **hold this close**.*
this was meant for you.

for the one i meet at moonlight
this is all of me in daylight.

endearment

i can tell

you are going to be the words
i've never had before.

it was lust at first sight.

one glance and i was out of my mind
so i passed you by.

i told myself
if this is meant to be
there will be another time.

blatantly daring fate to prove it.

because i heard
       what's meant to be will be
so what's a little dare
       to the powers above me.

if i am truly meant for you
nothing will keep me.

i had a beautiful dream
vivid and saturated
with your colors.

my imagination runs wild with you.

you're the light that guides my wandering eyes
and i can't bear to lose sight of you.

i found you in the dark
and our souls danced to the music
you played for us.

when we met the edge
you turned to me and said

    let's jump.

    we can just fall into each other
    forever.

i had promised myself
i would learn to love your soul first.

as they say
what's inside cannot lie.

-that will keep me safe. right?

i have never known another lover
to dance with me as you do.

i have only known
running in and running out
as fast as i can
before the light comes up
and they see me
for who i really am.

today i found myself
in the corner of your room

and this shell
that i have been dragging
door to door
felt a home

and found itself

whole.

(sleeping with a stranger)

he said

every day i will remind you
to reach for my hand
so that i may fall deep into your arms.

i just want to be
a blissful weight on your shoulders.

(spell casting)

now i miss the morning every day when noon hits.
the morning light greets us through the blinds
and he lets out a sigh.

there is something about his whine
and complaints of the hour
and nothing feels quite the same
as being kissed by the sun
together.

if young love were a letter
it would read

to the perfect man,

until life has outgrown us
you will never want or need of anything.
you will have without question
and all of me will always be
for you.

love,
a wide-eyed daydreamer

she likes to think she will exist
in the last second of his day
everyday.

that he would find her there
the first second
he was blessed with another
and maybe
they will create
a forever.

(picture perfect)

he whispered

why don't you just come here?

entwine your mind with my thoughts
wrap your arms around me
lace your fingers between mine.

you're the only thing
that holds me
together.

(playing cat & mouse)

now it might be too soon to say
but i like the weight of wearing you.

it might be too soon to say
but maybe i could leave myself behind
if that means you'll stay.

(chameleon)

they call me **naive** but

i pity the world
if there truly is

      only

      one

      you.

he just gives me that anxiousness.

the kind that begins in the depths of my body
and vibrates to the surface of my skin.

-when the butterflies in my stomach chant your name

i just want his hands
to hold the pieces of me together
so i don't lose myself

    or his grasp.

maybe that's too much to ask.

       (~~healthy~~ obsession)

some days he is no more than
a shadow on the wall that i will endlessly admire.

he holds a special place there
and the light will forever
shine toward him.

-heaven knows i wouldn't want to risk changing him

i'm just the girl who builds a life with you
in her head

              after you leave her

      day dreaming in bed.

some days i want him to be more
than just a visitor.

some days i want him to keep me
like i'm being held prisoner.

i've always been the person that people cling to
when they taste the love and admiration
i've been too willing to give.

they have their fill
and wander off into the daylight
until they hunger for more
under the moonlight.

-have i found another blood sucker in you?

to me
you are the color of bubbles in the sun.

-and now that i think about it i wonder
how many eyes have been as mesmerized by you
as mine have?

it's just the way you stare
with your bottom lip tucked behind your teeth.

i hunger for the taste of you.

*-but deep down i know
you might have your mouth full
of someone else*

call me crazy

but i just want to fill
all of the silence surrounding me
with your name.

-where have you been?

it's always on my mind.

that moment in time
when you looked down into my eyes
and i found myself

    falling

        into a pool of feelings
        you gave me to swim in.

(drowning in lust)

i come in and out of your life
like the sun and the moon.

no matter.

routine is just what i wanted to be.

if only you knew what i would give
to be the habit you never second guess.

i wonder if my pen will bleed the same shade
when your presence is no longer distant.

-will i have words when love is so close?

didn't i tell you?

i don't want to live in a world
where we don't die together
          after we collide.

the truth is
i want to wrap myself in you

but i know i would spread you
                    too thin.

today i wanted to tell you

for all of my nights
i'll dream beside you until we wake

and

for all of my days
i'll walk beside you until we lay.

-today i wanted to tell you

the sun was highest in the sky
when they found me frolicking
through your fields.

i heard them call me

the girl he schedules into his nights
after he's done
with his afternoon delights.

(cat's out of the bag)

now i know why
you remind me of a garden.

chaotic. overgrown. wild.

now i know why
you remind me of a garden.

*-you'd let any snake make a home
under the rocks in your flower beds*

i told him i had heard it all before.
what's the point in wasting time on apologies
that lead to goodbyes.

then he pulled me in and whispered

*i love the sound of only your leaves
blowing in my wind.*

and in that second
my head had no idea
where my heart had been.

(enchantment)

he whispers his
    sweet nothings

and i ~~choose to~~ forget
    his shortcomings.

(fool me once)

it's not the first time
i've asked myself

*where do you go
when you are lost in him?*

-it won't be the last

i have to confess

he is the sound that matches
the quake in my heart
and when he holds my hand i feel safe

even in his wild.

everywhere and anywhere with him
is a place i long for.

(entranced)

i feel your touch
when the wind runs past me.

it must be something about you
that grounds me
and keeps me from falling.

-or maybe i was taught to remember
if i stray too far your hands will find me

now we float through the air
riding on unspoken words
and a glance or two
here and there.

but soon
we will have to come down

and where
do we go
from there?

(magic carpet rides)

i will stay here

just in case you decide
i'm worth returning to.

just in case you decide
i feel like home.

i think we are a pair
you and i

afraid to be what we see.

we might be related to inevitability
and everyone knows
blood will always be thicker than water.

(generational curses)

it's true

i wonder if i'm
unworthy.

it's true

i wonder if i'm
out of place.

the more i think about it
i wonder what your love would feel like
if it were honest.

the more i think about it
i wonder what your love would feel like
if it were only mine.

Infatuation

can i tell you a secret?

the moon told me to leave you.

-but the sun is out now

he lights me on fire

with all intention of watching me burn
and still

his presence feels better
than my solitude.

(bonded to trauma)

so i asked

can't you shelter me from the rain
and take a bolt of lightning for me too?

or is it too much of me to ask
for you to hurt for me
the way i do
for you?

(givers & takers)

he didn't have to answer.

i knew he'd say

*we live in a world
where love doesn't leave you
begging for round two
quite like heartbreak does.*

i guess i should know better
than to ask questions i know the answers to.

i guess when you feel warmth
you don't always realize
the true intention
of the fire.

these chains make a beautiful sound
when you pull me in.

it almost distracts me
from the pain of being bound
to you.

(captive)

they are a ~~delusional~~ dreamy bunch
    my heart
    and
    my head.

my heart says
    i'll meet him anywhere at moonlight.
    our memories are vivid in darkness.
    we danced around time until it tired
    and left us shimmering until sunrise.

and my head interjects
    what a burden
    to bare the memory that lingers.
    how i dread the absence of him
    in daylight.

the truth is
i love when you hide from me.

there is something exhilarating about fearing
i might not find you.

(truly, madly, deeply)

it is pitiful
really

      how i envy the wind.

      but it's the only touch you allow
      with no question of intent.

you still move me
like we have been partners in this dance
for all of our days.

but there is music humming in the background
and it seems i always find the men easily swayed
to another rhythm.

(backup dancers)

he's the type of person who loves
to *love* everyone.

the more love he receives
the more *worthy* he is.

the more love he receives
the more *entitled* he is.

(god complex)

by now even i started to ask myself

how many red flags have you seen go by?

i tell myself
i'm not asking for much.

i just want this stillness
that continues to escape me.

i'm not asking for much.

just a bit of stillness
before the heartache comes.

(hold me until the inevitable)

i told him before

when you are done splashing in rivers

leaving stains on the concrete

i will be the ocean
waiting for you.

-i told him before i knew better

i'm in love with being the girl
who is searching for you.

if you ever stood beside me
i wouldn't know who to be.

(identity crisis)

maybe i am not everything **i could be**
because i am tangled in all of **your** *"could be"*.

i just wish your words had a mind of their own.

i hate how you speak for them.

if they made it to me before your restraints
we would be a story they have never heard of.

(alexithymia)

he said

i'm afraid.

i'm afraid to proclaim love.

in my mind it sounds like i'm screaming profanity.

i replied

*you want to know
what i'm afraid of?*

*i'm afraid you'll go looking for us
when the price of love has to be paid
and nothing has been saved.*

-just tell me you love me before it's too late

it's always the same.

i fall into your lust at first sight
and when you're done with me
i carry the burden of every goodbye.

and i still call you love.

-why?

even when he walks away
his body still talks in the language we made.

(snake charmer)

he would tell me

i prefer you scream your thoughts.

i can't feel your whisper.

i screamed
and i cried.

i cried
i won't let you end me
a thousand times.

but then i turned around
begging to be your beginning
all over again.

(cursed)

and here you are

knowing you are going to live forever
on these pages
and yet you still have no time

to offer me

to wipe my tears
to dry my eyes
to hold me
to tell me it's all just been a disguise.

to tell me anything
anything at all
besides these lies.

dear future self,

forgive me for this.
his eyes were so easy to fall into.

his hands were placed perfectly around my face
to carry my mind toward his.

(apologies in advance)

his memory makes me wander
through the streets of the world we built
and i wonder if he's been there since.

i wonder where he is.

i step thousands of times
trying to find that moment in time
where i was a part of his mind.

and i wander through the night
where we were most bright

where i know i will follow you
for the rest of my life.

(walks down memory lane)

i asked my soul not to give up on me
as she strained to pick up the pieces
you ripped out of me today.

she said

i won't beg you
i won't plead.

i just hope you find the version of you
that you love most.

maybe then you will hold onto yourself
and leave him to bleed.

the truth is i fell for him
and i haven't gotten up since.

i've been here

fooling around in a bed of weeds
disguised as bedded flowers.

(perfume potions)

do you know how the sight of you
holding a cigarette burns a fire inside of me?

you don't hold me that way
like my presence is a habit you never want to break.

even if it kills you

slowly.

now we've met too many times.

like my lips to my teeth and tongue
i have savored you for too long.

i spend too much time in reminisce.

the years have felt like moments
as i have lived with plenty of distractions.

my mind comes back to you countless of times
and i don't mind.

the truth is
there's too much comfort in the familiar.

(in and out of relapse)

don't you know
i live here?

this place you visit in loneliness
this place where you belong.

why don't you escape your mind
and stay the night?

there's no place
like home.

(habitual ritual)

can i tell you a secret?

i've had negotiations with the moon
to stay out a bit longer when we were together.

in exchange it kept my secret
and told me
i should know better.

now his soul lies where my skin sleeps.

even when he's not here i feel him
seeping into the space between these covers.

our memories will never wither.

they will blend in with egg shell shades
and sleep in cracks of dried paint.

-if these walls could talk they would mock me

now silence sings a song no other can sing.

at the most restless of times
i turn to the memories of our rhythm and blues
and i rise to dance with the shadows of you
that wander through our home.

(dancing with a devil)

i've blamed you for losing my mind
      but that never helped me find it.

i came back to you everyday
      begging you to tell me
      where you left it.

and there i go **again**

turning your way
and begging
for the time of day.

-is this madness?

deep down i know
we can't make a **home** under these covers.

but there is enough of you
and enough of me
to play **house** for a little while.

this is the insanity of people who love.

we dare to dance to sounds louder
than our own voices
and then wonder why we don't know
who we are.

put your heart in my body bag.

that's what he said but

i heard *hello again* instead.

(the hunted)

he really could destroy me
and make me believe he's healing me.

-and i'm terrified that i'm not terrified

i know we are meant to be a tragedy

but every second leading to the end
let's just call this
serendipity.

-i'm not through with lying to myself yet

i will never rid myself of you will i?

you are in the air of all the places i love.

like a candle that has burned too long
and all i smell is smoke.

there is no path when you walk away from me.

search and you will find
there is no escape from your need of me.

said the boy
who ate my breadcrumb trail.

(sabotage)

so my soul asked me

are you really in pain?
or are you playing along in a game?

(breaking point)

disdain

that damn moonlight made me a fool for you

and i've got questions.

all of these questions
like

what is love?
and
why are you never the answer?

all of these questions
just to force the idea of you
        out of me!

we don't drink the same water.

you bathe in this pool of feelings
that i drink from
until i drown.

you said you would teach me
how to swim.

(liar liar)

i met
surrender once

and he cursed me
for calling him love.

he told me
you never call your lover
your desires name.

(fantasy vs reality)

now look at what you've done to me.

i am a flower you keep covered in glass
with my petals scattered and spread
withered and split.

how could you leave traces of me
here and there
tainted with oil from the tips of your fingers?

now they find me incomplete.

bound to all of the lies that live here.

(what men do with their trophies)

i asked him
why?

to which he replied

**you are not whole
and you cannot fill yourself with me.**

(ignite)

now my rage makes me blind.

**now you've got your hands on my mind
and i never said you could fucking touch me.**

what a cruel joke this is.

what a cruel joke
to give the entire ocean to someone
who doesn't know how to swim.

you are the thorn in my side
that i should have picked off the stem
when i had the chance.

i ran so willing into that bush
just to be pricked by you.

now you're an open wound.

a void i cannot fill.

now you won't be able to hide them from me.

those small lies that slither
through the cracks of your teeth.

the wider you open your mouth
the more obvious your poison becomes.

(snake)

you were a name no one i knew associated with love
and that truth should have been enough.

(mirror mirror)

the problem was
you were the road less wandered
and i let that sway me.

-fairytales made a fool out of me

i'm stolen art.

i will no longer be held captive by you.

no longer will you put me on display
and use words of affirmation
to make me forget
why i wouldn't want to stay.

(approaching hells gate)

the truth is some men never want you around
but you're not allowed to leave them either.

so his nature caught wind
and his desperation exclaimed

wait!
do you remember that night in the park?
i picked your petals so selfishly.
the oil from my hands stained each piece of you
and when the last petal fell i told you
you'd love me.

i couldn't have been more wrong
than to put that curse on you.
i'm sorry.

(tactics of a manipulator)

silly boy
two can play this game.

i replied

how's this for a curse?

*the rest of your days are going to go by
without the sound of my voice
and the years may move at a normal pace
but i promise you*

*everyday will feel like an eternity
without me.*

(words can kill)

i swore
the last time was the last of this.

to leave you in reminisce
would be my legacy.

to leave you
would be my **beginning**.

i would rather

-forget how to breathe
-go through the shock of gasping for air with no relief
-die clutching my throat in the panic of suffocation

than live another day inhaling this life with you.

with you
i have lived in an asylum.

a place you built for me
with the imagination
of happiness between us.

it crumbled
delusion by delusion

consumed me
piece by piece.

i am so much better than this.

i am so much better than
the taste left underneath your tongue
but you deserve nothing more
than to feed off of the memory of me
forever.

(power)

in this life i have lived and died
a thousand times.

too many times you have
sifted through me
in your mind.

the worst part of it all is that

you gave me this space
that i don't feel good enough to stand in.

the worst part of it all is
i let you.

i fight it

the vulnerable part of me
that still wonders

if i had held you longer
would you have felt more like home
or just shelter?

-there's a difference

now even my dreams are
uncalled for temptations.

the remnants of your passion still
touch me in my dreams and wake me out of my sleep
to the emptiness of this bed and a memory.

-i'm still fighting to let go

i just couldn't stand it!

having my hands full of everyone else

but a mouth full of you.

as i release this pain in my heart
i know each word will give you more power.

but surviving this hurt is a strength
you will never conquer.

-you are not the alpha here

we meet and noise fills me.
what a curse to be haunted by the sound of us.

(toxic daydreams)

you wrote **remember** on my mind
and now i can't forget a fucking thing.

(cruel parting gifts)

when i heal
these letters will end
and your nights
will never be the same.

can you sleep without your lullaby?

-asking for a friend

i hate to remember him.

it's an unsettling memory
with a small light between us.

he filled my lungs with secrets and
told me silent stories in a kiss.

now he lives where my memories are
and i hear him knocking
before his hands touch the door.

(the guest who overstays his welcome)

there is something about this space.

this empty space between
  you
    and
  me.

there used to be a feeling there
and now
whatever it was
i just can't quite remember it.

    -distance makes the heart grow distant

you took the beauty out of the sound of my name.

nothing sounded sweeter.

now i can't bare the sound of their calls.

i wish i saw that beautiful part of me
before i let you take it
before i let you throw it away.

i wish i saw just one beautiful part of me.
i would have held myself closer
i would have kept you at bay.

enough is enough.

you will never know the anguish
you put me through
and i will never forgive you
for not asking.

(the end is near)

i had to stop arriving

with the same goodbye.

so i left him there
under our moonlight
with my

love me
&
love me not's

in the park.

(flowers & freedom)

soon you will be everything
i need you to be.

-soon you will be nothing

soon i will be all
i need to be.

-soon i will be everything

i want you to know that
i'm keeping these memories.

i know a moment will come
when i need to remind myself
why you are no longer
my home.

all of my pieces are bound in this book
*and here you are **again***
holding me in your hands
like you own me.

no matter.

i just want to know how deeply it kills you
to know that so many others
have had their fingers
in between these pages.

i just want to know

how deeply

it kills you.

midnight

for the one i meet at moonlight

pick up the phone

we have words to throw around.

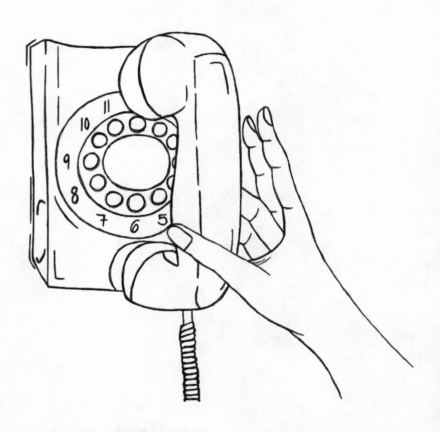

i have decided

this is where i will lay us to rest

*because i want to make peace
with the fact that **we** only belong
in memories.*

think of this as our coffin.

all that i gave
blood and bone alike
will lay here
with my memory of you.

the parts of myself that you manifested
that you influenced
that i don't want to claim or recognize
will be left here to die
so that i may live.

my soul must learn
to lose itself
to find where it is best kept.

so if actions speak louder
then i hope this hole in the ground
screams the grief
that i have been swallowing

because to you words mean nothing.

to you a hello is nothing without a touch
a goodbye is nothing without a kiss
and a good night is nothing without a rhythm
and drink in hand
so eventually i was nothing
if all i gave you was a thought
an idea or a story
from time to time.

i had to be more of my body
and much less of my mind.

so now i will bleed my words into
thousands of pages because i've decided
that my words will scream louder
than any of your worthless actions.

i know by now you might be weary
but i'm far past worn out.

i spent our time being dragged on the floor
by your shoe strings.

collecting the debris you left behind
to patch my wounds before you could see them bleed.

like scars could ever be trophies.
like i could clench this rubble of memories
into my palms and grind them into nothing.
like a glass house isn't exactly what i am
even though i want to be known as the stone
that shatters this to the ground.

although we
crumble and crush the rubble
we are still left
with the same weight in dust.

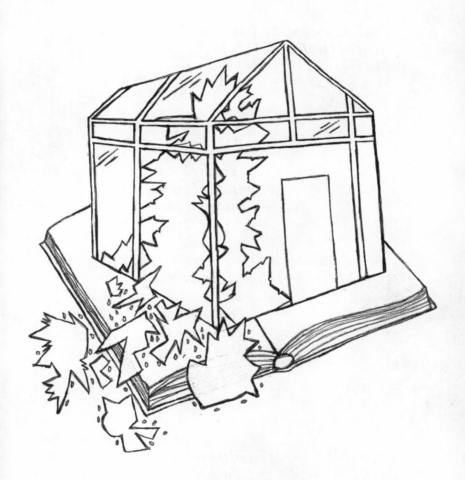

oh i am tired.
tired of being opened and closed
stretched and spread
like the spine of this book.

i am tired
of the misuse of my name
and the misuse of my love.

i am tired
of throwing madness into the air like confetti
and calling it showers of love.

i am tired
of searching for a breath in this suffocation
while you call it a virtue of patience.

oh i am more than tired
of all of these words i wish i could say
i would be numb to the next day
or the day thereafter.

can i tell you a secret?
i called this devotion.
forcing myself in like the wind under the door.
convinced myself that space was left there
as an open invitation.

can i tell you a secret?
this all sounds like fun and games.

obstacles and puzzles
hide and seek
king of the hill and capture the flag.

i guess i'm adolescent with my love
and i might be attached to pulling
at your imaginary strings.

can i tell you a secret?
Harley made me a fool
and not every Joker
will pull you out of the acid
you're willing to drown in.

they say
if you wanted to
you would
so now i know exactly why you didn't.

for me you were my only way.
for me your name remained
like it was the only thing i would ever need to say.

for me i thought i found a home
that one time i looked your way.
for me life was new and i prayed
it would never be the same.

for you this was all just one big play
and i'll take your silence as applause
because you've always known
just how to make my heart ache.

they said
if he wanted to
he would
so now i know exactly why
i can't anymore.

think of this as our coffin.

where i bury everything i had
and welcome in all that i lacked.

where i bury my anger
and welcome my peace.

where i bury my ignorance
and welcome my wisdom.

where i bury the weight of you
and welcome the relief in my soul that i need.

think of this as our coffin
where i bury us
and unearth all of me.

i have no more time
to waste on a single thought
of who you should have been.

i made it here.
i made it this far.

all that there is
and all that there will ever be
is me.

Victoria Pizzirusso

a note from the author:

if you found this i want you to know that
love is worth it.
we learn everything we need to about
ourselves when we love.
the hard parts make us strong
and the good parts make us gentle.

the secret is to love yourself first.
be whole and content with your own love.
dependency of others distracts you
from achieving the peace and happiness
that you deserve to have within yourself,
that you can discover within yourself.

time is too short to waste on looking
for something within others that you
already have inside of you.

-victoria

thank you for building this bond with me.
thank you for picking me up and
taking me in.

find more of my work and more of my love
on Instagram @wemeetatmoonlight

Printed in the USA
CPSIA information can be obtained
at www.ICGtesting.com
LVHW040037050624
782283LV00012B/20